THE
BEGINNER
ART BOOK
FOR KIDS

THE
BEGINNER
ART BOOK
FOR KIDS

Learn How to Draw, Paint, Sculpt, and More!

Daniel and Korri Freeman

ROCKRIDGE
PRESS

For general information on our other products and services or to obtain technical support, please contact our Customer Care Department within the U.S. at (866) 744-2665, or outside the U.S. at (510) 253-0500.

Rockridge Press publishes its books in a variety of electronic and print formats. Some content that appears in print may not be available in electronic books, and vice versa.

Interior and Cover Designer: Suzanne LaGasa
Photo Art Director: Sara Feinstein
Editor: Jeanine Le Ny
Production Editor: Edgar Doolan
Photography: © 2019 David Lewis Taylor, cover, p.ii–iii, 2, 6-7, 12-13, 36-37, 60-61, 78-79, 88, 96-97, 108-109, 128; Shutterstock, p. viii; Daniel and Korri Freeman, p.22, 31, 39, 41, 45, 49, 53, 57, 63, 65, 67, 69, 71, 73, 75, 80-87, 89-94, 98-105, 111, 113-115, 118-119, 121, 125.

Author photo: © Liz Chrisman Photography

Illustration: © Elizabeth Graeber, p. 4, 9-11, 35, 59, 77, 95, 107, 127, 134.

ISBN: 978-1-64152-412-4 | eBook: 978-1-64152-447-6

For our Finnli

CONTENTS

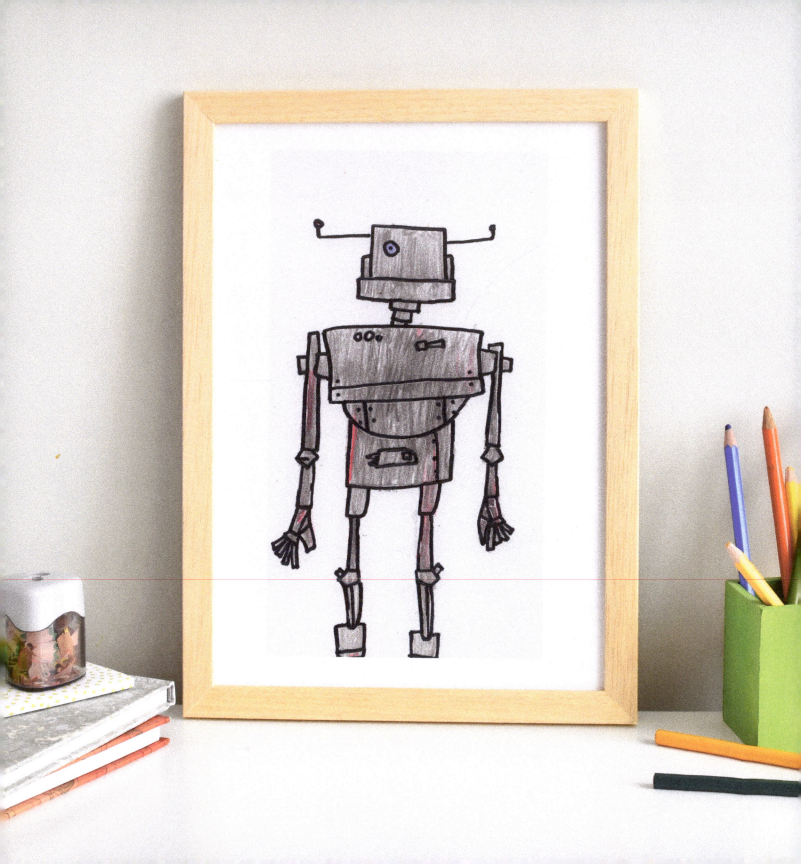

INTRODUCTION

Welcome to *The Beginner Art Book for Kids*! We're Daniel and Korri Freeman, a full-time artist and an art teacher. We own and operate KaleidoKids Art Studio in Arkansas, as well as an art gallery called Kaleidoclasm. We're so happy that you've chosen this book to use as a tool for artistic creation and inspiration.

Inside, you will find 46 super fun, simple projects for beginners to get your mind into the creative mode. Follow each project step by step, or use our instructions as a launch for your own original work. Either way, you will create art—even if you've never done it before!

The projects are divided into chapters based on medium, or how they are made. We've included projects for drawing, painting, sculpture, printmaking, found-object art, and mixed media. You'll print patterns with spaghetti, paint using cotton swabs, and even create your very own sketchbook.

Sometimes artists try really hard to create something special and then don't love the result. That's *okay*! Try again, or move on to a project you think you might enjoy more. Art is not always about the product; it's about what you learn in the process. Maybe you'll discover a type of art you never knew existed, or maybe one of our projects will inspire you to develop a new art form. Each artist has their own special way of doing things—including *you*.

HOW TO USE THIS BOOK

There are no rules in this book.

The projects in each chapter are organized from easiest to hardest, and you can begin your artistic journey with any one of them. Follow the instructions . . . or create your own version of the work. If one piece suggests using colored pencils and you would rather try oil pastels, go for it! Use this book as inspiration to make the kind of art *you* want to make.

Move through this book at your own pace, taking lots of breaks or working on more than one piece of art at the same time. And remember to check out the Advanced Art options for each project. These will give you even more ideas and show you how to push yourself to the next level.

TOOLS AND MATERIALS

Basic art supplies are easy to find, and they don't have to be pricey. You can find everything you need at your local department store or art supply store. You might even have some art supplies already in your home.

Each project in this book begins with a list of tools and materials that you will need. Here, we've listed the most common ones that you might be reaching for again and again. Keep an eye out for the ❗ next to certain tools, which means that you'll need an adult's help or extra supervision.

ESSENTIAL SUPPLY LIST

Black permanent marker

Brayer or foam roller

Cardboard

Colored markers

Colored pencils

Craft glue

Craft knife ❗

Eraser

Hot glue sticks

Low-temp hot glue gun ❗

Oil pastels

Paint (acrylic, tempera, watercolor)

Paintbrushes (different sizes)

Paint tray or palette (a paper plate or an egg carton works well, too)

Paper (drawing, watercolor, mixed media, scrapbook)

Pencils (#2, 4B or 6H)

Ruler

Scissors

Sharpener

Sponge

Tape (masking and washi)

A Paper for Every Project

We'll be using lots of different kinds of paper for the projects in this book. Here's what makes each one special:

Drawing paper is thin and useful when you're only using pencils, markers, or colored pencils.

Watercolor paper is thick and works well when you're painting with watercolors, or using oil pastels.

Mixed media paper is also thick, and is perfect for when you want to use a mixture of materials, or maybe even create a collage.

Scrapbook paper is a thin, decorative paper that has a pattern printed on it and can be used to add a colorful pop to your project.

What's the Point of Pencils?

Regular #2 pencils will work fine for the projects in this book, but if you want to try an artist's tool, look for a set of drawing pencils.

Drawing pencils have a letter and a number on them, such as "4B" or "6H," which tell you how hard or soft the graphite is within each pencil. Soft graphite (the "B" means black) makes darker marks, hard graphite (the "H" means hard) makes lighter marks, and the higher the number the harder or softer the graphite will be.

What's the difference between tempera and acrylic paints?

Tempera paint is perfect for beginners. It's usually washable, and it is great for learning to mix colors.

Acrylic paint is similar to tempera paint, but it is thicker and more permanent.

PaintBrushes

It's helpful for an artist to have a variety of brushes on hand to make their paintings rich and interesting.

Flat brushes are great for outlining things and filling in large areas.

Round brushes work well when you're adding details.

Small brushes are used for painting tiny details.

Large brushes are for painting bigger areas.

Don't forget to rinse and wash your brushes after every use!

Masking Tape versus Washi Tape

Masking tape is plain, colored tape that is great for holding things together temporarily.

Washi tape is a patterned tape that can be used as decoration on any artwork, or used as a tape when you need something less sticky than regular tape.

ORGANIZATION AND CLEANUP SUPPLY LIST

It is so much easier to create more artwork when you can come back to a clean space, rather than having to clean up before you start. Here are some supplies you'll need for keeping an organized and clean area.

★ Jars, boxes, or containers to store small objects and found materials

★ A large box or shelf to keep your papers and/or sketchbooks organized

★ Plastic tablecloth or newspaper to cover your workspace

★ Paper towels

★ Rags/sponges/wet wipes

MAKE YOUR OWN "CREATE SPACE"

Before you get started, make sure you have a bright, clean, and comfortable place to work. A kitchen table works great, or maybe even an open area on the floor or in your backyard. Here's a checklist to prepare your space for creating:

* Cover your work area as well as the floor around you with newspaper or a plastic tablecloth.

* Read the list of materials needed for your project and gather your supplies.

* Keep cleaning supplies on hand for quick cleanups.

* Wear a smock or "art clothes" that you don't mind getting messy.

ARTIST TIPS & TRICKS

Use these 10 tips and tricks to help you stay focused and positive as you create.

1. Keep a sketchbook and a pencil close by. You never know when you may get an awesome idea.

2. Pay attention to your surroundings. Notice the art in your everyday life and get inspiration from people and things that you see.

3. Take the time to study an object before you begin to draw it.

4. Sketch out your ideas before you begin a project.

5. Draw lightly. If you make a mistake, it's easier to erase.

6. If you make a mistake that you can't fix, don't start over. Instead, use your mistake and create something new.

7. Take care of your art supplies—especially paintbrushes. Always rinse them when you are finished using them.

8. Don't compare yourself to other artists. Only compare your artwork to your older artwork. That way, you'll see how much you have grown and improved.

9. Be patient. Good artwork takes time, so don't rush yourself.

10. If you don't like your artwork when you are finished, try again or move on to something else. Keep creating!

Chapter 1

Drawing

Drawing is the perfect place for a beginner to start because it is the foundation of everything. In this chapter, you'll learn some important skills and techniques—including how to create simple line drawings and how to use basic shapes to build an object—and you'll get to make lots of cool pictures! Draw a few doodles to get your creativity warmed up. Practice is key whenever you try something new. Once you feel comfortable with the basics, try one of our Advanced Art ideas—and add new ideas to the drawings to make them yours!

"I am always doing what I cannot do yet, in order to learn how to do it."

—Vincent Van Gogh

Robot Ralph

Messy Meter: ① ② ③ ④ ⑤

We love robots. There are so many ways to make them. Our friend Ralph might seem hard to draw at first, but if you can draw rectangles, circles, squares, and semicircles, then you can draw him. Give it a try!

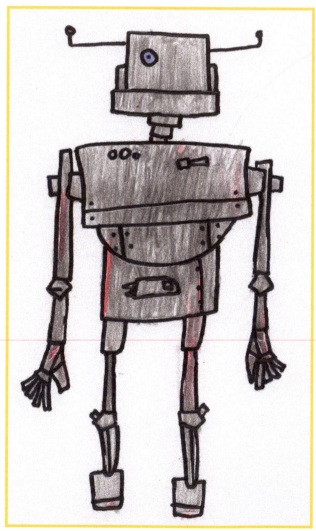

by Jett F.

WHAT YOU NEED:

* Drawing paper
* Pencil
* Eraser
* Black permanent marker
* Colored pencils or markers

WHAT YOU DO:

Draw steps 1 through 9 to create Ralph. Outline your robot with a black permanent marker, and then add color.

Advanced Art

Create a robot family using different shapes, sizes, and details so that each one is unique.

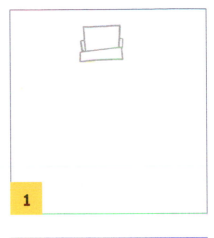

1

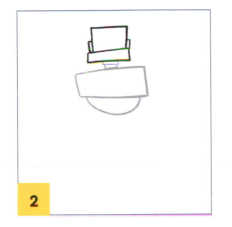

2

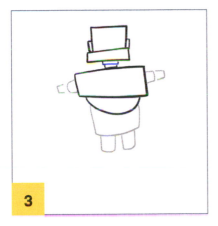

3

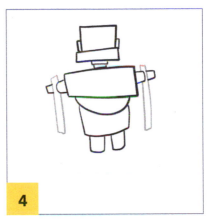

4

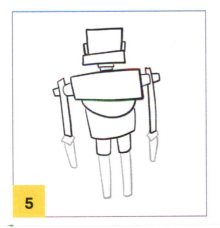

5

6

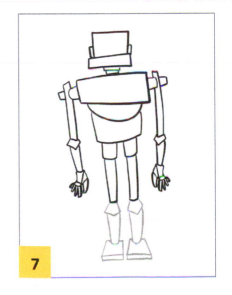

7

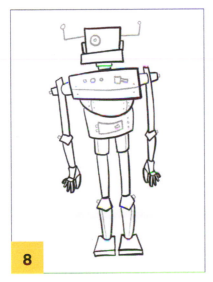

8

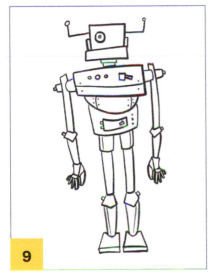

9

A Wise Owl

You can also use basic shapes to draw animals, like an owl. Owls have very large eyes and a flat face, which makes them extra fun to draw.

Advanced Art

by Ella I.

WHAT YOU NEED:

* Drawing paper
* Pencil
* Eraser
* Black permanent marker
* Colored pencils or markers

WHAT YOU DO:

Draw steps 1 through 8 to create an owl. Outline your owl with a black permanent marker, and then add color.

Advanced Art

Imagine where your owl lives. Does it live in a house? Is it perched in a tree? Draw a background for your owl.

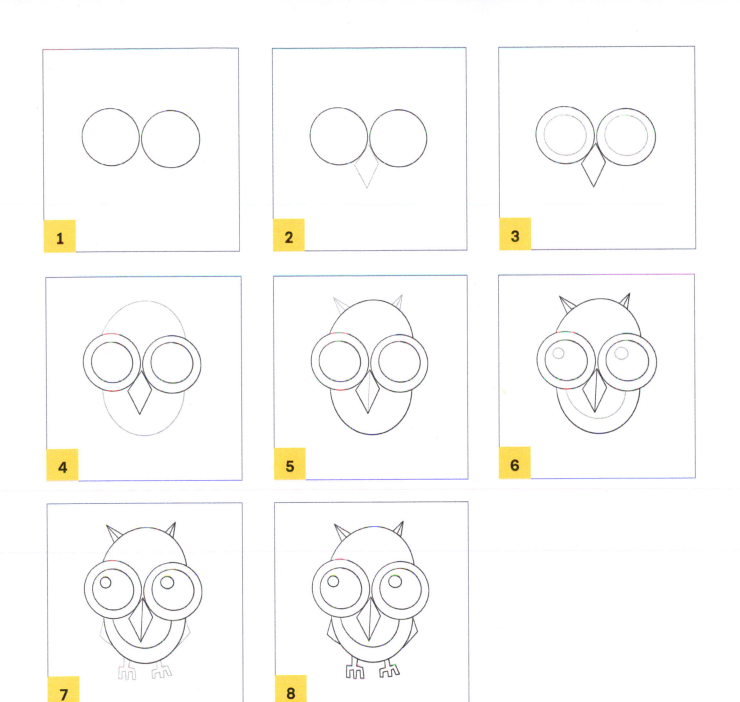

Fun Bunny

Messy Meter: ① ② ③ ④ ⑤

Organic shapes can have a curvy and flowing form, such as the shape of a leaf or the outline of a rock. We used lots of organic shapes to create this rabbit. Try it out for yourself, and then see what other animals you can draw using organic lines and shapes.

by Jett F.

WHAT YOU NEED:

* Drawing paper
* Pencil
* Eraser
* Black permanent marker
* Colored pencils or markers

WHAT YOU DO:

Draw steps 1 through 8 to create a rabbit. Outline your rabbit with a black permanent marker, and then add color.

Advanced Art

Try drawing a picture using *only* organic shapes and lines (no circles, squares, triangles, etc.). It's not as easy as it seems!

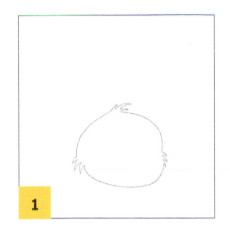

1

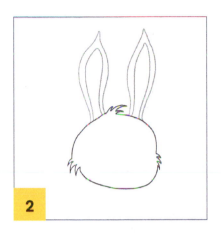

2

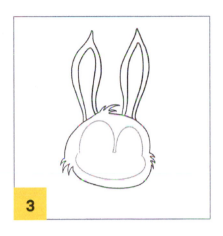

3

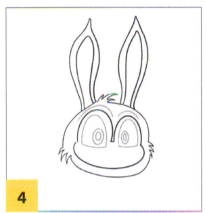

4

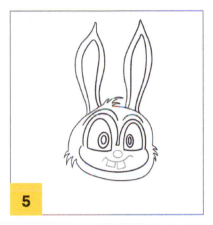

5

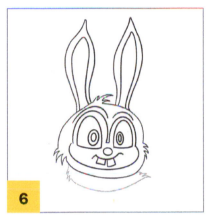

6

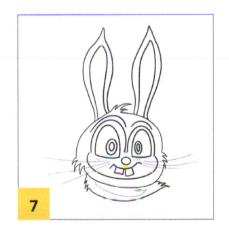

7

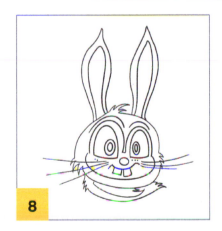

8

colorful contours

Contour line drawings focus simply on the outline and shape of the object that you are drawing, not on details like shading. You can create contour line drawings of anything you can think of: books, flowers, fruit, stuffed animals, even art supplies.

by Jett F.

WHAT YOU NEED:

* Objects to draw (see above examples, but they can be anything!)
* Scrap paper
* 11-by-14-inch drawing paper, any color
* Pencil
* Eraser
* Black permanent marker
* Colored pencils, markers, or oil pastels
* Scissors
* Craft glue

WHAT YOU DO:

1. Draw a few practice sketches of each object. We chose a paintbrush, pencil, bottle of glue, scissors, ruler, and paint palette.

2. On your sheet of drawing paper, use contour lines to draw only the outline of each object. Be sure to overlap your drawn objects, so that nothing is floating around by itself on your paper.

3. Outline your drawing using a black permanent marker and then use markers, colored pencils, or even oil pastels to add color. If you used brightly colored paper, feel free to leave some spaces uncolored so that you can see your background color.

4. Cut out your drawing and glue it onto different colored paper so that it really pops!

Advanced Art

Poke a pencil through a paper plate and then try drawing the objects again. You won't be able to see what you're drawing, which will help you focus on following the contour lines of each object.

symmetrical Crowns

Messy Meter: ① ② ③ ④ ⑤

When something is symmetrical, it means that it is the same on both sides. Let's learn about creating symmetry in art with this symmetrical crown design.

Advanced Art

by Ella I.

WHAT YOU NEED:

* 18-by-12-inch mixed media paper
* Ruler
* Pencil
* Eraser
* Scissors
* Hole punch
* String

WHAT YOU DO:

1. Use a ruler to draw a straight line all the way across the bottom of your paper. This will create the base of your crown.

2. Find the center of the line. Draw a dot several inches above that point, however tall you want your crown to be, but save a little room at the top of the paper.

3. Add a few dots to the left of the center one. They can be different heights. Do the same on the right. Try to make the left and right sides look symmetrical.

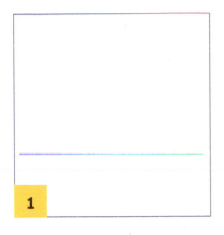

1

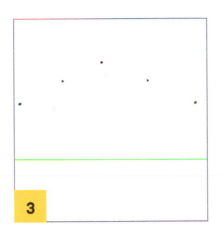

3

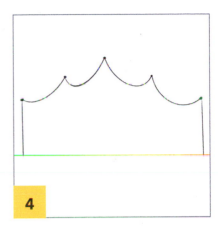

4

4. Draw curved lines (or any kind of lines) to connect your dots. This will form the top of your crown.

5. Now draw some jewels on your crown. Make sure your jewel design is the same on both sides.

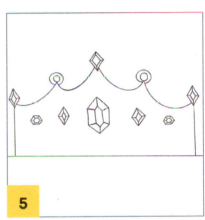

5

6. Cut out your crown, punch a hole on each end of the base, and add a piece of string to each hole to tie the crown around your head. Wear your crown with pride.

Advanced Art

Use acrylic or tempera paint to add color to your crown. Once your paint is dry, outline it with a black paint pen or permanent marker.

self-Portrait

Messy Meter: ① ② ③ ④ ⑤

Creating a self-portrait may seem scary, but as long as you are brave enough to try and you have a mirror, you can do it. It's all about drawing what you *see* and not what you *think* you look like.

by Jade L.

WHAT YOU NEED:

* 11-by-14-inch sheet of mixed media paper
* Mirror
* Pencil
* Eraser
* Colored pencils
* Oil pastels
* Black colored pencil

WHAT YOU DO:

1. Draw your head. Start with a simple oval. Draw a very light line down the middle from top to bottom, and then do the same thing from left to right.

2. Draw your eyes on the horizontal middle line and your eyebrows, too. With each step, be sure to look at your face in the mirror and focus on the feature that you're about to draw next.

3. Draw your nose halfway between your eyes and your chin.

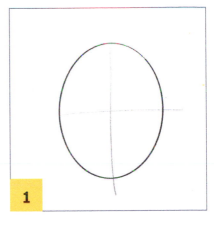

1

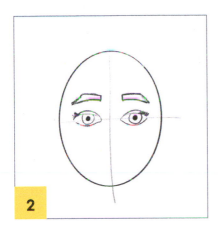

2

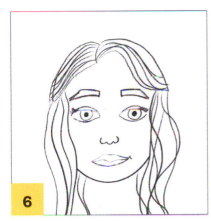

3

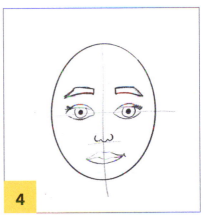

4

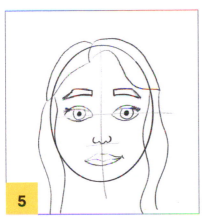

5

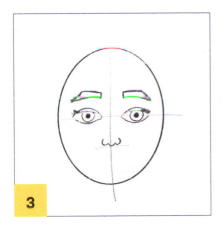

6

4. Draw your lips halfway between your nose and your chin.

5. Draw your hair, but make sure you start your hairline below the line at the top of your head.

6. Erase any lines you don't need anymore, then add your neck.

7. Add color to your self-portrait with colored pencils or oil pastels. Then outline your portrait with a black colored pencil.

Advanced Art

Draw your family and friends. Have someone sit down across from you so that you can spend some time drawing them.

SCALE UP, SCALE DOWN

Messy Meter: ② ③ ④ ⑤

What is scale? It's the size of an object when compared to other objects. Some artists make large-scale drawings, like huge murals on the side of a building. Others draw very small-scale on tiny pieces of paper. In this project, you will be practicing scale by drawing a small object bigger than it really is.

by Ella I.

WHAT YOU NEED:

* A small object (such as a key, feather, or screw)
* Drawing paper
* Pencil
* Eraser
* Black permanent marker
* Colored pencils
* Scrap paper
* Black colored pencil

1

2

WHAT YOU DO:

1. Draw the object, and make it as big as you can. You can even make it go off the page a bit if you want.

2. Outline your drawing with a black permanent marker and color it in with colored pencils. Make it very colorful and be creative.

3. On a sheet of scrap paper, try drawing some patterns that you might like to use for your background. Use a simple pattern so that it doesn't distract from your object, like stripes or polka dots. Then draw it on your picture and color it in.

4. Create even more depth by adding shadows around your object to make the background look farther away. Draw this by using a black colored pencil and lightly coloring around the edges on one side of your object.

Advanced Art

Now let's create a small-scale drawing. Choose a large, detailed object to draw as small. Keep your pencils sharp so you can draw even the tiniest of details.

Continuous Flower

Messy Meter: ③ ④ ⑤

Continuous line drawing is when you don't pick your pencil or pen up off your paper the entire time that you're drawing. With continuous lines, you can look at your paper as much as you want and take your time. Just make sure not to pick up your pencil. (If you do, that's okay! Just put it right back down where you left off.) Don't be afraid of making "random" lines through your drawing; that's what makes this technique stand out.

WHAT YOU NEED:

* Flower (or picture of a flower)
* Drawing paper
* Pencil, pen, or black permanent marker

Advanced Art

Repeat this same exercise multiple times on one piece of paper, letting your drawings overlap each other.

WHAT YOU DO:

1. Look at a flower and decide what area you will start drawing first. Place the tip of your pencil on your paper, making sure that you have plenty of room all around to draw.

2. Start drawing slowly, while looking at the flower every few seconds to see what you should draw. Look at each part as you draw it.

3. Before you pick your pencil up, do a quick check to be sure that you didn't miss anything important. If you did, go back and add it without lifting your pencil from the paper.

by Maci C.

Panel Drawings

Messy Meter:

Over a thousand years ago, stories were told through a series of images called panel paintings. Art was created on different pieces of wood and then connected so that together they told a story. Think of a story you could tell using drawings. You will create multiple small drawings that are separate, but fit together— almost like a puzzle. You can also draw one object that stretches across all of the pieces, or a scene with different characters in each piece.

by Jett F.

WHAT YOU NEED:

* Scrap paper
* Pencil
* Eraser
* Five 5-by-5-inch sheets of drawing paper
* Masking tape

* Scrap cardboard, at least 30 inches wide
* Black permanent marker or pen
* Colored pencils
* Colored markers

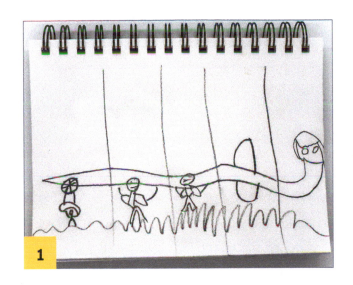

1

4

WHAT YOU DO:

1. Think about a picture or a story that you could create on multiple panels. Maybe you have characters that are human, or maybe they're all animals. What are they doing? Divide your scrap paper into five sections and sketch out some ideas.

2. Line up the 5-by-5-inch sheets of paper in a row on top of the scrap cardboard. Use masking tape to tape down the borders of each sheet to keep them still while you draw.

3. Draw your scene onto the 5-by-5-inch sheets of paper.

4. Outline your drawing with a black pen or permanent marker and then add color. We like to use colored pencils for small spaces and markers to fill in larger spaces.

5. Trace around the inside of your masking tape with a black permanent marker to create a border, and then carefully peel the tape off.

QUICK TIP

To avoid accidentally ripping your art when you remove the masking tape, make it less sticky by sticking it to your shirt or pants before taping it to your paper.

Advanced Art

Write a story to go with your illustrations, and then mix up the order of your drawings and see if the story changes.

How to Draw a 3-D House

Messy Meter: ① ② ③ ④ ⑤

When you draw a house, does it usually look flat, or two-dimensional? We'll show you how to add depth to your house to make it look three-dimensional.

Advanced Art

by Jade L.

WHAT YOU NEED:

* Drawing paper
* Pencil
* Eraser
* Black permanent marker
* Colored pencils or markers

WHAT YOU DO:

Draw steps 1 through 9 to create a 3-D house. Outline your house with a black permanent marker, and then add color.

Advanced Art

Give your house a story. Where is your house? What is around it? Draw the scene.

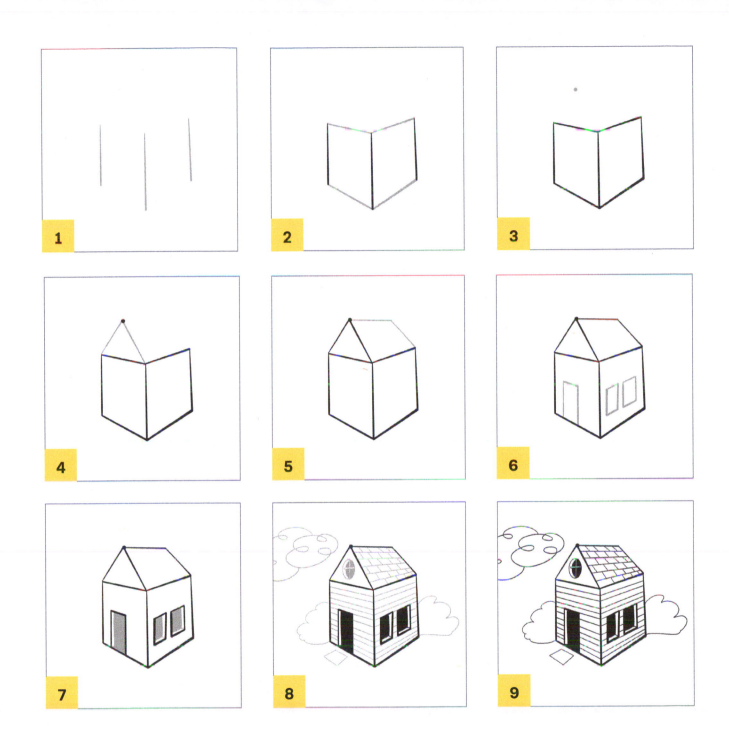

MORE DRAWING IDEAS

1. See how many things you can draw on one sheet of paper in a certain amount of time (one minute, 30 seconds, etc.). Remember, it's easier to draw an object if you can look at it closely.

2. Find a toy or action figure in your room. Draw it in a unique setting and create a backstory.

3. Grab a friend or a family member. Sit across from one another at a table and draw each other at the same time. Add color with colored pencils or oil pastels.

4. Write down five random words, put them in a bowl, then choose three of them. Create and draw a character based on those three words.

5. Make a continuous line drawing that includes at least five objects. Remember not to pick up your pencil between objects.

Chapter 2

Painting

Painting can be a fun and sometimes messy activity to do when you're feeling creative. You can paint on paper or a canvas, as well as other things such as a piece of wood, a rock, or even an old T-shirt! The projects in this chapter use watercolors, tempera, and acrylic paint. You'll learn how to make creative paintings, discover fun ways to mix colors, and gain the inspiration you need to start your own new projects.

"I am happy to be alive as long as I can paint."

—Frida Kahlo

Splatter Painting

Messy Meter: ① ② ③ ④ **5**

Let's get messy! Splatter painting is a great way to loosen up and relax before a more detailed painting project. There are no rules to splatter painting, and there's almost no wrong way to do it.

by Maci C.

WHAT YOU NEED:

* Plastic tablecloth or newspaper
* A canvas or mixed media paper, any size
* Acrylic or tempera paint in a few colors of your choice
* Cup for each color of paint
* Cup of water
* Paintbrushes, 1 inch or wider

Advanced Art

Cut a heart out of contact paper, place it in the center of the paper or canvas, and then splatter paint on top. Remove the contact paper once your paint is dry to reveal your sweet design.

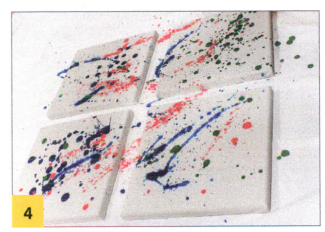

WHAT YOU DO:

1. Prepare your painting area by laying down a large plastic tablecloth or lots of newspaper. This project is best done outdoors, where you can move and splatter freely.

2. Lay your canvas onto your painting area and get your paints ready. You want your paint to be thin so that it's easy to splatter. Put some paint in a cup, add a small amount of water, and mix it up. Do this for each color.

3. Dip your paintbrush into the watered-down paint. Then hold your brush up high and swing it down toward your canvas. If your paint is drippy enough, get a big bunch on your brush and simply hold it over your canvas and let it drop down to make big splotches.

4. With a loaded paintbrush, hold it still in one hand while tapping it with the other hand to create smaller splatters.

watercolor Still Life

Messy Meter: (1)(2)(3)(4)(5)

Have you ever seen a painting of a bowl of fruit or a vase of flowers? That's called a still life. When you paint real objects that are in front of you, instead of from a picture or your imagination, that means you are painting from life. Let's try it out!

WHAT YOU NEED:

* Objects for still life (such as books, stuffed animals, a lamp, or anything you want)
* Paintbrushes, small round and large flat
* Watercolor paints
* Cup of water
* Watercolor paper

Advanced Art

Once your paint is dry, look at your objects again to see if you can find any small details. Use a small brush to add in any details that you find interesting.

WHAT YOU DO:

1. Arrange the objects you've chosen on a table. Try stacking two objects on top of one another or having the objects overlap in the front and back.

2. Start with a round paintbrush and activate your watercolors by adding a little bit of water and scrubbing it around gently with your brush.

3. Now start painting what you see! Don't worry about messing up. If you make a line that's in the wrong place, just leave it there and make a new line.

1

by Jade L.

Painting Puzzles

Messy Meter: ① ② ③ ④ ⑤

Putting together a puzzle is such a fun way to study a piece of artwork. You really get to experience the shapes and colors as you piece it together. Let's make our own.

by Maci C.

WHAT YOU NEED:

* ★ Mixed media paper or cardboard
* ★ Pencil
* ★ Tempera or acrylic paint
* ★ Paintbrushes
* ★ Paint palette
* ★ Black permanent marker or paint pen
* ★ Ruler
* ★ Scissors or a craft knife ❗

QUICK TIP

If you choose to work with cardboard, make sure you give both sides a solid coat of paint or primer to keep it from warping. Let it dry thoroughly before beginning the project.

1

2

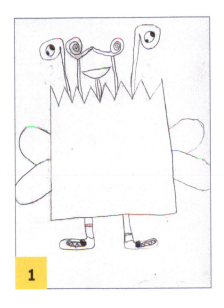

3

WHAT YOU DO:

1. Decide what you want your puzzle to look like and sketch it out with pencil on the paper. Be sure to add some details to the design. If it's too simple, your puzzle will be really hard to put back together.

2. Paint the sketch with tempera or acrylic paint. When it's dry, outline it with black permanent marker or a paint pen.

3. Flip the painting over and use a ruler to draw lines where you want to cut the painting into puzzle pieces. If your surface is really thick, like cardboard, have an adult help cut it with a craft knife.

4. Mix up the pieces and see how fast you can put the puzzle back together. If it seems too easy, cut it into smaller shapes.

Advanced Art

Add lots of intricate designs with markers or paint pens to make your puzzle even harder.

Shades and Tints in Fractured Circles

Messy Meter: ① ② ③ ④ ⑤

We love experimenting and mixing paint colors. Adding black to a color creates a shade, which is a darker color. Adding white makes a tint, which is lighter. In this project, you will learn how to create shades and tints of any color of the rainbow.

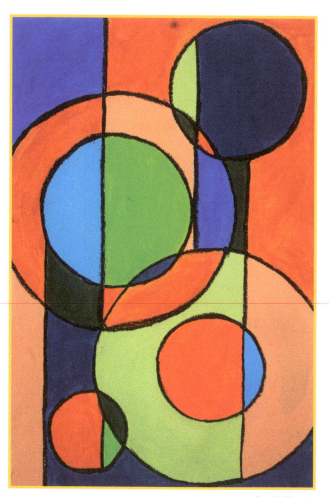

by Keller W.

WHAT YOU NEED:

* Watercolor or mixed media paper
* Circular objects to trace (lid, cup, jar, bowl, etc.)
* Pencil
* Eraser
* Ruler
* Tempera or acrylic paint in white, black, and your choice of colors
* Paint palette
* Craft stick
* Paintbrushes, small round
* Cup of water
* Black oil pastel or paint pen

WHAT YOU DO:

1. Trace a variety of different-sized circular objects on your paper. Make it interesting by overlapping them or even drawing circles inside of other circles.

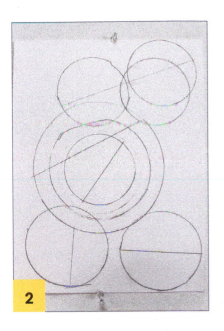

2. Next, use a ruler to draw straight lines though your circles, breaking them into sections. Keep in mind that you will be painting each section, so keep them fairly large.

3. Pour a small amount of the same color paint in three different sections of your palette. In the first section, add a little bit of white paint to create a lighter tint of your color. Start small, mix it with a craft stick, and then add more white if you want it to be lighter. In the second section, mix in a small drop of black paint to create a darker shade of your color. Black is very strong and will change the shade of your color quickly, so use it sparingly.

4. Do the same with as many colors as you would like. We used three colors: blue, orange, and green.

5. Use your original and new colors to paint your fractured circles. Be careful to stay inside of the lines. Once the paint is dry, outline each section with a black oil pastel to make your shapes pop.

Advanced Art

Use only one color for your whole piece. Create as many tints and shades of the color as you can. Then fill in your shapes and outline each section.

Shape Animals

Messy Meter: ① ② ③ ④ ⑤

In the style of art called Cubism, painters used a lot of geometric shapes to create the images in their paintings. We will be using a Cubist approach in this project to create our own work of art.

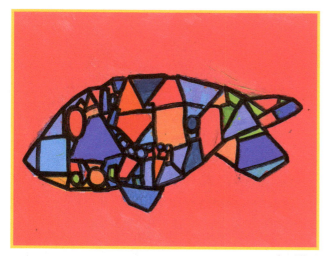

by Ella I.

WHAT YOU NEED:

* ★ 9-by-12-inch sheet of mixed media paper
* ★ Pencil
* ★ Eraser
* ★ Ruler
* ★ Paintbrushes, small round
* ★ Tempera or acrylic paint in black, white, and your choice of colors
* ★ Paint palette
* ★ Cup of water
* ★ Black oil pastel, paint pen, or marker

1

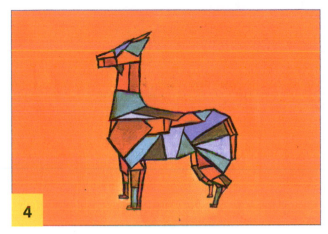

4

WHAT YOU DO:

1. Draw any animal on your paper, and then see how you can break it up using squares, circles, diamonds, triangles, etc. Draw the shapes right on top of your sketch. We chose a llama and broke it up into shapes using a ruler. Our student, Ella, chose a fish.

2. Add color to each shape, using tempera or acrylic paint. Use lots of colors. You can even mix tints or shades of some colors using white or black to create more variety.

3. Choose a color to paint your background. Choose one that is either lighter or darker than most of the ones you've already used to make your animal really stand out.

4. Once your paint is dry, use a black oil pastel, paint pen, or permanent marker to outline your shapes. We used a black paint pen.

Advanced Art

Add some texture and highlights to your piece. Rub similarly-colored oil pastels on some of your painted colors, while being careful to stay inside the lines. Use the tip of a white pastel along corners and edges to add glimmers of light.

warm & Cool Cutouts

Messy Meter: ① ② ③ ④ ⑤

Did you know that some colors are considered *warm*, and others are considered *cool*? Warm colors include red, orange, and yellow. Cool colors are their opposites: green, blue, and violet. For this project, we will create and combine two separate pieces of art—one warm, and one cool.

by Keller W.

WHAT YOU NEED:

* Two sheets of mixed media paper
* Pencil
* Eraser
* Tempera or acrylic paint in your choice of colors
* Paintbrushes
* Cup of water
* Scissors or a craft knife ⚠
* Glue

WHAT YOU DO:

1. Draw a full-page patterned background with a pencil on a sheet of paper.

2. Carefully paint in your design using warm or cool colors and let it dry.

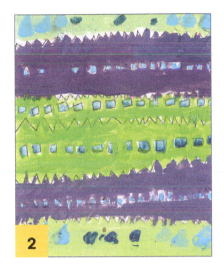

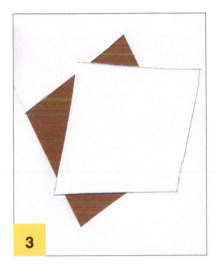

3. Draw a shape (diamond, heart, triangle, etc.) or a simple design in the middle of a second sheet of paper. Make it big and bold. In the space around your drawing, paint with the colors you haven't used yet. If you started with warm colors, now use cool colors, and vice versa.

4. Once your second piece is dry, have an adult help you cut out the big design you drew on the middle of the page.

5. Layer your cutout piece on top of your background piece. Notice how the colors show through the cutout section? Glue the top piece onto the bottom piece.

Advanced Art

Make the top layer pop even more by inserting some small cardboard spacers between the two pieces and gluing them together. You can also sharpen the details by outlining your patterns with a black permanent marker or paint pen after the paint has dried.

Painting Your View

Messy Meter: ① ② ③ ④ ⑤

When you look out your window, what do you see? Maybe you see tall buildings, a row of houses, or beautiful scenery. Choose one object and create a piece of artwork based on it, either on how the object really looks or how you would like it to look.

WHAT YOU NEED:

* Scrap paper
* Pencil
* Eraser
* 8-by-10-inch or larger sheet of mixed media paper
* Tempera or acrylic paint in white and your choice of colors
* Paintbrushes
* Paint palette
* Cup of water

WHAT YOU DO:

1. On scrap paper, practice by sketching an object you see outside of your window.

2. Now, use acrylic or tempera paints to create your object without drawing it first on mixed media paper. This will be a challenge, but it will give your piece a great, painterly look. Make sure to paint the object big, so that it fills most of your paper. This object is your focal point.

3. Once you have your general outlines, start filling in each part of your object. Use solid colors first, and then let it dry. Don't be afraid to use lots of colors or to be creative and make your object a different color from what it really is.

4. Create a simple background so that your object can stand out. You may choose to paint the real object's background, or you can make up your own.

5. Once your paint is dry, use white paint on a small paintbrush to add highlights and details to your object. Look at your object to find bright spots, then add a touch of white where you see them.

Advanced Art

Instead of paint, use black charcoal or chalk pastels to add shadow, or white pastel to add highlights, and make your painting stand out even more.

by Jett F.

Pointillism Painting

Messy Meter: ① ② ③ ④ ⑤

Pointillism is a fun painting technique that uses dots instead of regular brush strokes, giving it a totally different look, feel, and texture than other types of painting.

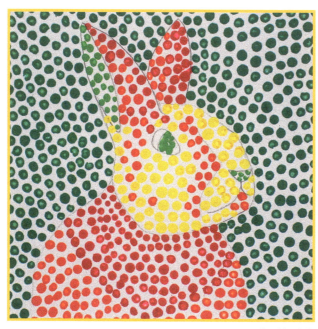

by Maci C.

WHAT YOU NEED:

* 9-by-12-inch or larger mixed media paper
* Pencil
* Eraser
* Cotton swabs
* Tempera or acrylic paint
* Paint palette

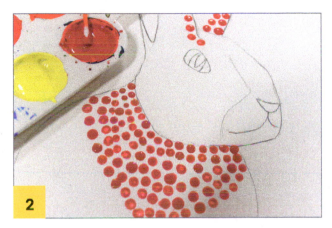

WHAT YOU DO:

1. Draw an image on your paper very lightly using a pencil. Dip a cotton swab into the paint color you would like to start with and begin filling one section of your drawing with dots. You will have to redip your cotton swab every now and then to add more paint.

2. Fill in each section with the colors of your choice. You can spread your dots out so that they don't touch or add lots of dots to any areas that need more color. Make sure to switch your cotton swab each time you use a new color!

Advanced Art

Create dots of different sizes by using different objects, such as the end of your paintbrush, the tip of a sharp pencil, or even a toothpick.

BLOCK-OUT Painting

Messy Meter: ① ② ③ ④ ⑤

A stencil is a great tool for an artist. It allows us to paint an image on top of something without worrying about it getting messy. For this project, we are going to make our own stencil and create some detailed designs.

by Jett F.

WHAT YOU NEED:

* ⭐ Two sheets of mixed media paper
* ⭐ Pencil
* ⭐ Eraser
* ⭐ Scissors
* ⭐ Masking tape
* ⭐ Paintbrushes
* ⭐ Tempera, acrylic, or watercolor paint
* ⭐ Cup of water
* ⭐ Black permanent marker

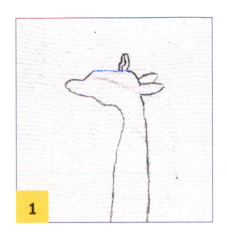

WHAT YOU DO:

1. On one sheet of paper, draw an interesting shape or outline. Keep it fairly simple.

2. Cut your paper exactly where you drew the lines, being careful not to snip off any other parts of the page. This sheet is now your stencil.

3. On the second sheet of paper, paint a background that goes with your stencil. For example, our student painted an African savannah to go with a giraffe stencil. Include lots of details.

4. Once your paint is dry, tape the stencil on top of the background. Place a few pieces of rolled masking tape onto the back of the stencil to stick it on temporarily.

5. Paint the opening of the stencil with the color of your choice.

6. Once your paint is dry, carefully remove the stencil and check out your creation. Outline your design with permanent marker so that it stands out against your background.

Advanced Art

Use stencils with acrylic or fabric paint to design T-shirts or canvas bags.

Collaboration— Painting with Friends

Messy Meter: ① ② ③ ④ ⑤

Drawing and painting with friends can be a great activity to practice teamwork. In this project, you can work with friends or family members to create a big collaborative piece of artwork that everyone can be proud of.

by Ella I., Keller W., Jade L., and Jett F.

WHAT YOU NEED:

* 18-by-24-inch or larger mixed media paper, corrugated cardboard, or canvas
* Paintbrushes, large (1-by-1.5-inches wide) and small
* Acrylic or tempera paint
* Cups of water
* Black permanent marker
* Paint pens
* Oil and chalk pastels

1

2

WHAT YOU DO:

1. Decide as a group what you would like the subject of your artwork to be. It could be a scene, or a large patterned piece. Then sketch your idea onto the paper, cardboard, or canvas.

2. Paint the big sections first and fill them in. Then use smaller brushes to paint the smaller spaces. Remember that this is a group project, so be respectful and supportive of your team members' decisions and discuss any changes you might want to make.

3. Once your paint is dry, add more color and details to your painting. Don't be afraid of messing up; if something happens that you don't like, talk to your team members about how you can fix it.

QUICK TIP

If you are painting on cardboard, make sure to cover the back with paint or primer first to prevent warping. Let it dry thoroughly before beginning the project.

Advanced Art

Before painting, add texture to your collaboration piece by gluing on pieces of scrapbook paper, tissue paper, or other materials. Be creative!

MORE PAINTING IDEAS

1. Create your own color wheel. Having a color wheel in your create space is a great way to choose colors for your artwork.

2. See what happens when you mix different colors together, then paint with them. Remember to make some tints and shades, too.

3. Use fabric paint to create a design on some canvas sneakers. Make sure to sketch out your design first.

4. Create a piece of artwork using only two colors that are complementary, or opposites, such as red and green, yellow and violet, or blue and orange.

5. Paint a self-portrait using only a paintbrush—no drawing first!

Chapter 3

Printmaking

Printmaking is an art form in which you apply ink (or paint) to one surface and then transfer it onto another surface, creating an image. A lot of things that you are familiar with—such as graphic T-shirts, magazines, and newspapers—were all printed. There are many different ways to make prints, and we will learn about a few of them in this chapter.

"It's good as an artist to always remember to see things in a new, weird way."

—Tim Burton

Spaghetti Prints

Messy Meter: ① ② ③ ④ ⑤

Hatching is a technique of drawing or printing closely spaced parallel lines to make a shading effect. It can also create a cool pattern. In this project, you will learn how to create a stamp that produces hatched lines out of spaghetti!

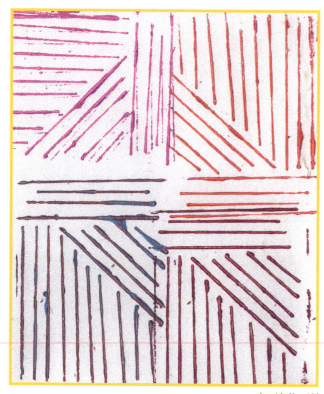

by Keller W.

WHAT YOU NEED:

* Three 3-by-4-inch pieces of scrap corrugated cardboard
* Uncooked spaghetti
* Craft glue
* Acrylic or tempera paint
* Paintbrush
* Small plate or bowl
* Mixed media paper

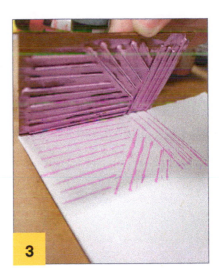

1 **2** **3**

WHAT YOU DO:

1. Break up the spaghetti into pieces short enough to fit onto the cardboard. Glue the spaghetti to your cardboard pieces and let it dry. This will be your stamp.

2. Pour some paint into a plate or a small bowl, dip your paintbrush, and lightly paint your stamp, making sure to cover all of the spaghetti pieces.

3. Print your design onto a sheet of mixed media paper or a primed piece of cardboard. Use as many colors as you want. Try to stamp your designs close together to create a pattern.

Advanced Art

Create more stamps with other items, such as yarn or rubber bands, using the same technique.

Quick Tip

Make sure that the spaghetti pieces are spaced apart and are mostly parallel. If you place them too close together, your lines will blend into each other and form a blob of paint.

Tape Resist Printing

Messy Meter: (1)(2)(3)(4)(5)

Sometimes artists want to get a little messy, but still need to keep certain parts of their paper or canvas clean. In this project, we will be making a polystyrene stamp print, and then using a tape resist technique to create a cool effect.

by Jade L.

WHAT YOU NEED:

* ★ 5-by-7-inch mixed media paper
* ★ Washi tape or masking tape
* ★ Polystyrene foam plate or takeout container
* ★ Pencil
* ★ Tempera or acrylic paint
* ★ Paintbrush, brayer, or foam roller

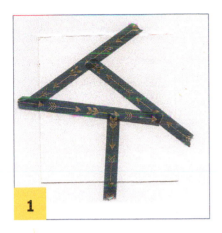

1

2

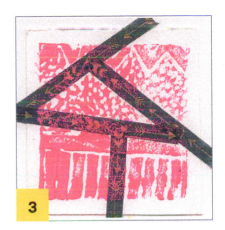

3

WHAT YOU DO:

1. Use the tape to create a design on the mixed media paper. Washi tape works great because it's not too sticky and will be easy to peel off.

2. "Draw" a design on your plate with a pencil. You want to press hard enough to make indentions on the polystyrene, but not so hard that it punches all the way through. This will be your stamp.

3. Use a paintbrush, brayer, or foam roller to add a thin layer of paint to your stamp. Press the stamp firmly onto your paper, right over the tape design. Be careful not to slide it across the paper and smudge the design.

4. Slowly peel your stamp off the paper to see the design.

5. Once the paint is dry, carefully peel off the tape to reveal your finished print.

Advanced Art

Try using different tape widths to add more variety to your design. Once you've removed the tape, use markers or paint pens to draw a pattern inside the white lines.

Patterned Roller Prints

Messy Meter: ① ② ③ ④ ⑤

Sometimes artists might need a pattern to cover a large area of their work. Here is a simple way to create a repeating pattern that doesn't appear to have a beginning or end, using materials you may already have at home.

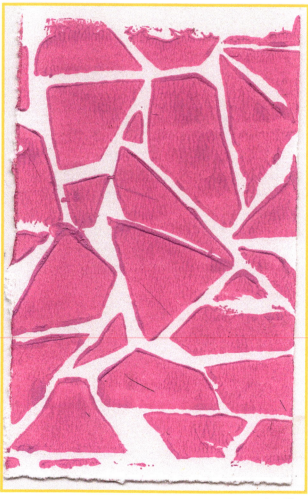

by Ella I.

WHAT YOU NEED:

* ★ Sticky foam sheets
* ★ Pencil
* ★ Scissors
* ★ Cylinder (paper towel roll, empty coffee can, etc.)
* ★ Eraser
* ★ Tempera or acrylic paint
* ★ Sponge or foam brush
* ★ Masking tape
* ★ 9-by-12-inch mixed media paper

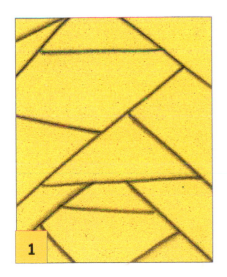

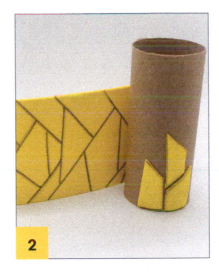

WHAT YOU DO:

1. Draw shapes on a sheet of sticky foam that you would like to incorporate into your design. You could use geometric shapes like squares and triangles, or even some organic shapes.

2. Cut out your design, peel off the backing, and stick each piece to your cylinder. Space them out so that the pieces don't touch. Cover the entire cylinder.

3. Add a light layer of paint to your patterned roller with a sponge, and carefully roll your cylinder across the page. Avoid smudging it as you go.

If you are using something hollow, like a paper towel roll, you can keep your fingers on the inside so that you don't get printed, too! Fill the page with your design.

Advanced Art

Once the paint is dry, outline shapes in your pattern and add details around your shapes using markers or colored pencils to create a cool, detailed piece.

Cardboard Relief Prints

Messy Meter: ① ② ③ ④ ⑤

A relief print is made from a surface that has some sections that are raised higher than other sections. The sections that are raised get ink and the lower sections get no ink. You will be creating your own relief print using pieces of recycled cardboard.

by Maci C.

WHAT YOU NEED:

* Scrap paper
* Pencil
* Eraser
* Two pieces of 9-by-12-inch or larger corrugated cardboard
* 11-by-14-inch or larger mixed media paper
* Scissors or craft knife ❗
* Craft glue
* Sponge, brayer, or foam roller
* Tempera or acrylic paint
* Markers, pens, or colored pencils

WHAT YOU DO:

1. Sketch out some simple design ideas on scrap paper. Pick the one you like best and redraw it onto a piece of cardboard. Make it big enough so that it is easy to cut out.

1

2

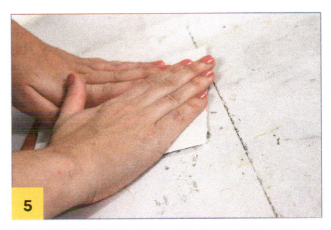

3

4

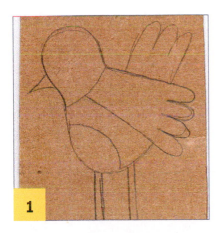

5

2. Ask an adult to help you cut out each piece of your drawing. Create texture on a few of your pieces by peeling away the top layer of your cardboard to reveal the ridges underneath.

3. Glue the cutouts onto a second piece of cardboard and let it dry. This will be your stamp.

4. Apply a thin layer of paint onto the raised cardboard using a sponge or brayer.

5. Lay a sheet of mixed media paper carefully on top of your stamp. Press down gently with your hands so that the whole page touches the paint. Be careful not to slide the paper or the paint will smudge.

6. Slowly peel your relief print off the stamp, then lay it out to dry. Once your relief print is dry, add details by outlining or adding patterns to the printed areas.

Monoprint Trading Cards

Messy Meter: ① ② ③ ④ ⑤

With most printmaking techniques, an artist is able to recreate the same print multiple times. However, with a monoprint, the print can be created only once. No two monoprints are the same. Let's print some one-of-a-kind trading cards that you can share with your family and friends.

by Jett F.

WHAT YOU NEED:

* Aluminum foil or plastic wrap
* Masking tape
* 11-by-14-inch sheet of cardboard
* Acrylic or tempera paint
* Paintbrushes
* Three pieces of 2.5-by-3.5-inch mixed
  media paper (trading cards)

WHAT YOU DO:

1. Set up your printing station by taping down a piece of aluminum foil to the sheet of cardboard. The foil should be big enough to create a few trading cards.

2. Paint a colorful design on your surface approximately the size of a trading card. Carefully lay your trading card facedown onto your painted design and press down. Be careful not to smudge it.

3. Slowly lift your card up from one corner and lay it out to dry. Now do a few more.

4. Once your cards are dry, add your signature and the date to the back of the card. Then trade them with your artist friends!

Advanced Art

Before printing onto your trading cards, give them a patterned background using paint or black permanent marker. Once you print over it, you may only be able to see it faintly, but it will add texture and dimension to your card.

Pizza Box Printing

Messy Meter: ① ② ③ ④ ⑤

This is one of our favorite activities because, well, we love pizza! We always have pizza boxes waiting to be recycled, so why not use them for an awesome art project instead of tossing them?

by Jett F.

WHAT YOU NEED:

* Pencil
* Sticky foam sheets
* Scissors
* Small recycled pizza box
* Mixed media paper (cut to fit inside the pizza box)
* Paintbrush, brayer, or foam roller
* Tempera or acrylic paint

WHAT YOU DO:

1. Draw a relief design on the sticky foam, cut it out, and stick it onto the lid of the pizza box.

2. Place a sheet of paper on a flat surface, next to your pizza box. Paint the foam relief design on the lid of your box, then open the box all the way so the lid presses down onto your paper to create your print.

3. Now you have an all-in-one printing station! Keep all your printmaking supplies inside the pizza box while you're on the go.

Advanced Art

Instead of using a small pizza box, use a big one so that you can create an even larger relief print.

Oil Pastel Monoprints

Messy Meter: ① ② ③ ④ ⑤

Although most printmaking techniques use ink or paint, we love using oil pastels in our studio to create prints with a unique texture. You will be using oil pastels to add color to one page, while drawing on the back of it to transfer an image on another page. The image you create will come out totally unique and have a great texture that you can't get by simply drawing with oil pastels.

by Maci C.

WHAT YOU NEED:

* Two sheets of 5-by-7-inch or larger drawing paper
* Oil pastels
* Masking tape
* Pencil

WHAT YOU DO:

1. Color one of sheet of paper completely with an oil pastel. It doesn't have to be totally solid; we used three layers of color. Use the pastel on its side to get more color onto the paper quicker.

2. Lay your two sheets of paper right next to each other, with your colored side facing down, and then tape them together using two small pieces of masking tape. Fold the two sheets together, like you're closing a book, making sure that the color is in the middle.

3. Draw a design on the back of the colored sheet. Be as detailed as you want. Press firmly with your pencil, but not hard enough to rip the paper.

4. Unfold the papers to see your monoprint, and carefully remove the tape. You can use your colored paper for multiple monoprints, and you can always add more color to it if you need to.

Advanced Art

Instead of using one oil pastel, use multiple colors to create a rainbow-like monoprint.

MORE PRINTMAKING IDEAS

1. Create a print on black paper using white paint, then add color with markers once the white paint is dry.

2. Use bubble wrap as a stamp to create texture on your artwork.

3. Create a monoprint by adding paint to a piece of smooth plastic, and then lay your paper on top.

4. Make your own stamps using air-dry clay.

5. After you have made your first print from any project, grab another piece of paper and without adding more paint, print again to create a "ghost print."

Chapter 4

Sculpture

A sculpture is any type of artwork that is three-dimensional, or has volume. It's one of the oldest known forms of art. Subtractive sculptures, often made from stone or wood, are the oldest and one of the most difficult forms of sculpture. When creating a subtractive sculpture, the artist takes away material using tools instead of adding other materials to create the form. We will be creating additive sculptures, or sculptures where we combine materials to create art, using a mixture of traditional sculpting materials, such as air-dry clay, and some recycled materials.

"Inspiration exists,
but it has to find you working."

—Pablo Picasso

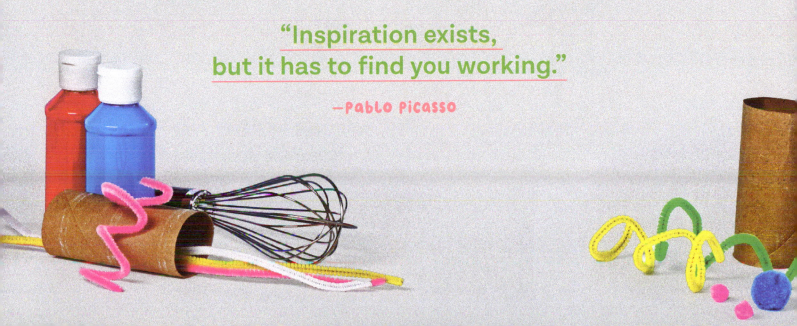

Wire Mobiles

Messy Meter: ① ② ③ ④ ⑤

A mobile is a three-dimensional hanging piece of artwork, just like what you might see above a baby's crib. You can create a mobile out of almost any materials, as long as they're not too heavy to hang. We will be using dowel rods and pipe cleaners to create this one.

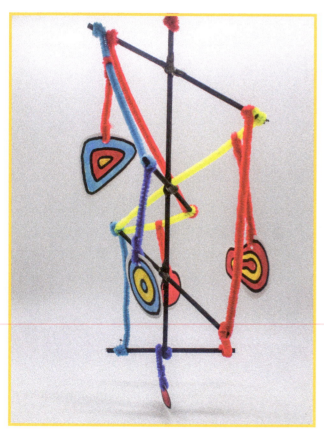

by Matthew C.

WHAT YOU NEED:

* One 12-inch wooden dowel
* Four 6-inch wooden dowels
* Low-temp hot glue gun ⚠
* Hot glue sticks
* Tempera or acrylic paint
* Paintbrush
* Sponge
* Wire or pipe cleaners
* Mixed media paper
* Pencil
* Eraser
* Markers
* Scissors
* Hole punch

WHAT YOU DO:

1. With the 12-inch dowel as the base in the middle, add the four 6-inch dowels to the sides using hot glue (ask for an adult's help), and let it dry.

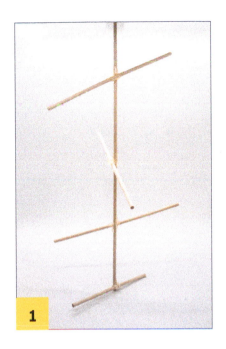

1

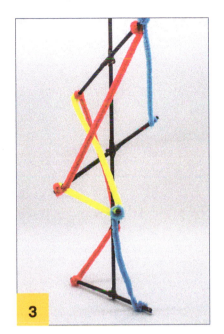

3

4

2. Paint your sculpture any color (or colors) you'd like. Use a sponge to get into the small cracks between the dowels.

3. Attach wire or pipe cleaners all around your dowels to add an interesting visual design.

4. Draw and color some small shapes or pictures on mixed media paper, then cut them out. You may want to add color to both sides of your cutouts. Punch a hole at the top of each drawing.

5. Use pipe cleaners to attach the cutouts to your mobile. Loop another pipe cleaner, and twist it around the top dowel, so you can hang your mobile.

Quick Tip

Wooden dowels are typically sold in a long length. Ask an adult to cut them down to the size needed. You can also have them cut at a hardware store.

Advanced Art

Instead of using dowels, use only wire to create the base of your mobile. Thinner wire is easier to bend, but if you want to use a thicker wire, needle-nose pliers would make it easier to shape.

Air-Dry Clay Bugs

Messy Meter: ① ② ③ ④ ⑤

Have you ever looked really closely at your favorite insect? In this project, we'll use air-dry clay to create your very own bug collection. You can make bugs that you've seen before or invent your own species.

by Maci C.

WHAT YOU NEED:

* Air-dry clay
* Toothpicks
* Acrylic or tempera paint
* Paintbrushes, small round
* Wire

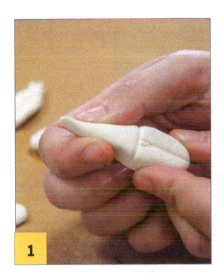

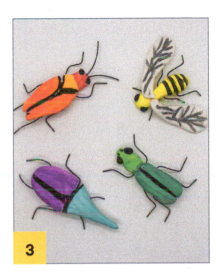

WHAT YOU DO:

1. Sketch out a few ideas, and then mold the clay into the shapes of your favorite bugs. Make sure your bugs aren't too small or too big; a clay ball about the size of a silver dollar works for making your bug's body.

2. After you have created several bugs, allow them to dry. This could take a day or two, depending on how large your bugs are.

3. Once your bugs are dry, use small paintbrushes to paint them. Add plenty of details to make your bugs beautiful.

4. Don't forget the legs! After your paint is dry, bend small pieces of thin wire into legs and push them into the body of the bug.

Quick Tip

Use something small, like a toothpick, to carve tiny details into the clay.

Advanced Art

Create a "Bug Board." Decorate the lid of a shoe box, glue your bugs on the inside, and even add name tags to identify each insect—whether real or from your imagination.

Recycled Cardboard Animal Sculpture

Messy Meter: ① ② ③ ④ ⑤

Think about your favorite animal: What shapes is it made of? Does it have wings? Big eyes or small eyes? What colors could you use to bring it to life? Got it? Now, let's turn it into a sculpture!

by Jett F.

WHAT YOU NEED:

* Pencil or marker
* Corrugated cardboard
* Scissors
* Oil pastels
* Low-temp hot glue gun ❗
* Hot glue sticks
* 12-inch dowel rod
* Polystyrene block, around 2-by-3-by-3-inches

WHAT YOU DO:

1. Draw the body of your animal on a piece of cardboard. Draw features such as eyes, nose, ears, whiskers, or anything else, separately.

2. Cut out the body and each feature, then layer them together to make sure they are the right size.

3. Use oil pastels to add color to each piece.

4. With an adult's help, use the hot glue gun to attach your pieces together, then glue a dowel rod to the back of your sculpture.

5. Add a big dot of hot glue to the center of the polystyrene block. Poke the dowel rod of your sculpture through the glue and into the polystyrene. Hold your sculpture still for a minute to allow the glue to dry.

Advanced Art

Consider how your sculpture looks from all sides. You may decide to add color to both sides so that it is interesting from all angles, or give your animal a tail, using either cardboard or pipe cleaners.

Recycled Skyline

Messy Meter: ① ② ③ ④ ⑤

If you could create your own city, what would it look like? Would you have lots of tall buildings, or more houses? Would it be painted with rainbow colors? Let's sculpt your unique vision with recycled objects and papier-mâché.

by Ella I. and Keller W.

WHAT YOU NEED:

* Recycled materials (bottles, cups, paper towel rolls, toilet paper rolls, etc.)
* Low-temp hot glue gun ⚠️
* Hot glue sticks
* Flour
* Water
* Large bowl
* Whisk
* Newspaper
* Tempera or acrylic paint
* Paintbrushes
* Water cup
* Decorative items: buttons, beads, washi tape, etc.

WHAT YOU DO:

1. Arrange your recycled materials to look like buildings standing beside one another. With an adult's help, use hot glue to attach them all together.

2. To make your papier-mâché paste, combine 1 part flour and 2 parts water in a big bowl. Use a whisk to mix it up until there are no clumps.

3. Cut the newspaper into strips, about 1 or 2 inches wide. Dip a paper strip into your paste, wipe off the extra paste, and stick it onto the "buildings" by smoothing it onto the surface. Cover the entire sculpture with glued strips and let it dry completely. This may take a few hours, depending on how many layers of paper you add.

4. Paint each building to create the city you imagined, and let it dry.

5. Add other decorations. You can glue on buttons or beads and paint doors and windows onto your buildings. Get creative with your city.

Advanced Art

Attach your cityscape to a base (a piece of wood or cardboard), and then make roads, stop signs, houses, and more to take your city to the next level!

circle Weaving

Messy Meter: (1)(2)(3)(4)(5)

Some artists use fibers, such as yarn or cloth, to create texture and patterns in their sculptures. This project involves weaving on a circular loom. Make as many as you can and attach them to each other to create an awesome wall hanging!

Advanced Art

by Jade L.

WHAT YOU NEED:

* 12-by-12-inch or larger corrugated cardboard
* Scissors
* Yarn; 5 feet in one color, 3 feet in three or four other colors
* Masking tape

WHAT YOU DO:

1. Cut a circle out of a piece of cardboard, around 10 to 12 inches wide. Cut an odd number of slits all the way around your cardboard, around 1 or 2 inches apart. We made 13 slits.

2. Take the 5 feet of yarn to create your warp, or base to weave onto. Secure the yarn to the back of your cardboard with masking tape. Then slide the yarn through one of the slits and flip your circle back to the front side.

3. Now take the yarn straight across the circle and insert it into the opposite slit. Repeat until you have gone all the way

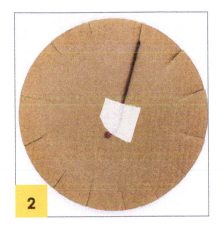

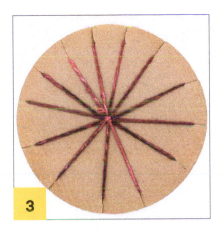

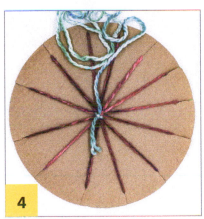

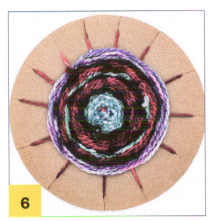

around the circle and each slit has one piece of yarn in it. The end of the yarn should now be on the front side of your circle. Use it to tie all the pieces of yarn together at the center of the warp.

4. Grab a different colored of yarn and tie it to the middle of your warp.

5. Weave in a circle by alternating the yarn above and below your warp strands. Don't pull too tightly. You want the yarn to lay flat and not bunch up.

6. When you run out of one color of yarn, tie another color on to the end and keep weaving until your loom is full.

Advanced Art

Color your cardboard loom with oil pastels before your begin weaving. Then add beads to your weaving as you go. Use scrap yarn to make pompoms, and tie them to your work for added dimension.

Toothpick Tents

Messy Meter: ① ② ③ ④ ⑤

Creating tiny sculptures is a fun way to practice a building technique. We love to build things, and toothpicks are the perfect tool for building miniature objects. If you want to scale this project up a bit, you can do this same process with craft sticks or dowel rods.

by Matthew C.

WHAT YOU NEED:

* 11 Toothpicks
* Low-temp hot glue gun ⚠️
* Hot glue sticks
* Paper
* Scissors
* Pencil
* Eraser
* Markers

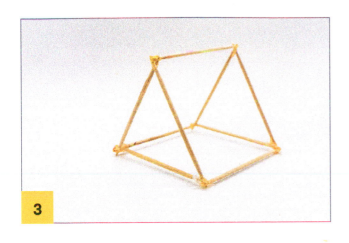

3

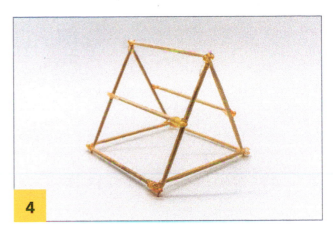

4

WHAT YOU DO:

1. With an adult's help, hot glue three toothpicks together, end-to-end, to create a toothpick triangle. Repeat this to make a second triangle and make sure to crisscross the ends.

2. Connect your two triangles by holding each one upright and gluing another toothpick straight across the top. Put a dab of glue in the spot where your toothpicks cross and set your new toothpick down in that section. Do the same on the other side.

3. Once that dries, flip your sculpture over and do the same on the other four corners.

4. To make it extra sturdy, glue another toothpick straight across the middle of two sides.

5. While your glue dries, cut a piece of paper that is the same width as your toothpick tent. Draw and color a design on your paper. This will be your tent cover.

6. Attach your tent cover by gluing it to one of your bottom toothpicks, wrapping it around the top, and gluing it again on the other side.

Advanced Art

Use the same technique to build other shapes, such as a square to make a house or a tall rectangle to make a building. You could even create an entire neighborhood!

Papier-Mâché Characters

Bring your own characters to life by using basic recycled materials and papier-mâché. Your character can be a human, an animal, or a creature of your own invention. Be sure to make a few sketches of the characters you would like to create before starting your sculpture.

by Matthew C.

WHAT YOU NEED:

* Newspaper
* Masking tape
* Toilet paper tube (or paper towel tube)
* Scrap cardboard
* Scissors
* Craft glue
* Low-temp hot glue gun ❗
* Hot glue sticks
* Dowel rods or sticks
* Flour
* Water
* Large bowl
* Whisk
* Tempera or acrylic paint
* Paintbrushes
* Cup of water
* Polystyrene for base, about 2-by-3-by-3-inches

WHAT YOU DO:

1. Create the head of your character by crumpling a piece of newspaper into a ball. Make it as big as you need to by adding more newspaper.

2. Wrap the ball in masking tape to keep it together, and then tape it to the top of the toilet paper tube. You can also add a similar crumpled ball of newspaper inside the bottom of your tube for extra sturdiness.

3. If your character has a nose or ears, add those by crumpling up smaller pieces of newspaper, or cut small pieces from cardboard and attach them with hot glue (with an adult's help).

4. Use dowels or sticks for your character's arms and legs. Ask an adult to attach them with hot glue.

CONTINUED >

PAPIER-MÂCHÉ CHARACTERS

5. Mix up your papier-mâché paste. Combine 1 part flour and 2 parts water in a large bowl. Whisk together until there are no clumps.

6. Cut newspaper into strips, about 1 or 2 inches wide. Dip paper strips into your paste, wipe off the extra paste, and smooth it onto the surface. Cover the entire surface in papier-mâché, including the arms and legs, and let it dry completely. This may take a few hours, depending on how many layers you have added.

7. Push the dowel legs into the polystyrene block so that your character stands up by itself. Brush on a base layer of white paint. Allow it to dry, and then paint your character's face, body, and clothes.

Advanced Art

Give your character even more personality. Use fabric to create an outfit or cover your character with short pieces of yarn to add fur. You can also attach other things such as googly eyes, feathers, or antennae to make your character look extra unique.

MORE SCULPTURE IDEAS

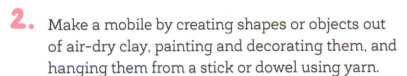

1. Create a sculpture using only paper and glue. Cut your paper into strips, then fold and bend it in different ways to make it three-dimensional.

2. Make a mobile by creating shapes or objects out of air-dry clay, painting and decorating them, and hanging them from a stick or dowel using yarn.

3. Make a papier-mâché bowl by blowing up a balloon and placing papier-mâché strips onto one half of the balloon. Let it dry and then pop your balloon. Add petroleum jelly to the balloon before you begin to make it easier to separate.

4. Build a movable sculpture. Form a stable base out of wire shaped like a stick figure, cover the base with layers or aluminum foil, and then pose your figure!

5. Make temporary sculptures using mini marshmallows and toothpicks. You can build anything!

Chapter 5

Found Objects

Look around you right now. What do you see? Maybe an old toy, some seashells from the beach, or maybe a few random buttons? In this chapter, we will be transforming everyday items like these—found objects—into works of art. So, start a collection of found and recycled objects you can use. You could even make a trip to your local thrift or junk store to look for some extra special treasures. Be sure to ask your parents for permission before you glue and paint objects found around the house.

Here are some examples of objects you might want to look for: bottle caps, old CDs, buttons, dowel rods, egg cartons, fabric scraps, metal cans, old keys, pipe cleaners, plastic bottles, pom-poms, ribbon, small toys or other trinkets, spools, springs, sticks, string, used plastic containers, wood pieces, and more.

> "Art is often created through the re-imagining of ordinary things."
>
> —Unknown

Found Object Trophy

Messy Meter: ① ② ③ ④ ⑤

Trophies come in all shapes, sizes, and shiny colors. Instead of making a trophy out of metal, we will build our own trophy from some found treasures. Think about what type of trophy you would like to create and who you may be creating it for—"Most Creative Artist," "Coolest Dad," "Best Friend Ever" . . . the possibilities are endless!

by Matthew C.

WHAT YOU NEED:

* Found objects from your collection
* A 4-by-6-inch wooden block, or any other shape
* Low-temp hot glue gun ❗
* Hot glue sticks
* White paint or primer
* Small bowl
* Sponge
* Metallic paint (spray paint works best)

Advanced Art

After the trophy is completely dry, add embellishments like yarn, ribbon, or pom-poms to create a more colorful and creative prize. Make and add a label saying what the trophy is for and then present it to a friend or family member.

WHAT YOU DO:

1. Choose found objects based on the type of trophy you want to create. For example, if you're creating a "Most Creative Artist" trophy, you might decide to use some old paintbrushes, pencils, or crayons.

2. With an adult's help, hot glue the largest found object to the wooden block. Once it's dry, glue on smaller found objects to build up your trophy. Keep in mind that everything will be one color in the end.

3. Pour white paint or primer into a small bowl and paint the entire trophy using a sponge to get into the hard-to-reach areas.

4. Let it dry, then apply the metallic paint. If you are using spray paint, have an adult do this part outside.

Creature Terrarium

Messy Meter: ① ② ③ ④ ⑤

Terrariums are glass cases or globes where you can display small creatures, bugs, or plants. They make for a beautiful display of a prized object. We'll be creating our own creature or plant from found objects, and then placing it inside a plastic "terrarium" for safekeeping.

by Maci C.

WHAT YOU NEED:

* Found objects
* Low-temp hot glue gun
* Hot glue sticks
* Tempera or acrylic paint
* Paintbrush, small round
* Paint palette
* Artificial or preserved moss
* 8-by-8-inch piece of cardboard
* Small rocks and twigs
* Scissors
* Two-liter plastic bottle
* Tacky glue

WHAT YOU DO:

1. Think of a bug, animal, or any small creature you could create using things from your found object collection. The only rule here is to make it small enough to fit inside your plastic bottle terrarium.

2. With an adult's help, attach your pieces to each other using hot glue. You may decide to paint your creature to add some recognizable details, or just leave it bare so that everyone can see the materials you used to create it.

3. Hot glue the moss onto your cardboard piece, and maybe add some small twigs or rocks to add a natural element to your terrarium.

4. Ask an adult to help you cut the top off a plastic two-liter bottle. The leftover bottom piece will be your "glass" globe.

5. Set your creature on your cardboard base. Use tacky glue around the edge of your two-liter bottle and place it carefully on top of your found object creation.

Advanced Art

Use recycled materials, such as egg cartons or cardboard pieces, to make some "plants" or "flowers" to add inside your terrarium for a pop of color.

small object mosaic

Messy Meter: ① ② ③ ④ ⑤

Most traditional mosaics use glass or ceramic tiles glued down to a flat surface in order to create a picture or a pattern. In this project, we will be creating a type of mosaic, but instead of using glass or tiles, we will be using small found objects.

by Maci C.

WHAT YOU NEED:

* Small found objects
* 11-by-14-inch piece of corrugated cardboard
* Pencil
* Low-temp hot glue gun ❗
* Hot glue sticks
* Craft glue
* Acrylic paint
* Paintbrushes
* Ribbon or pipe cleaner

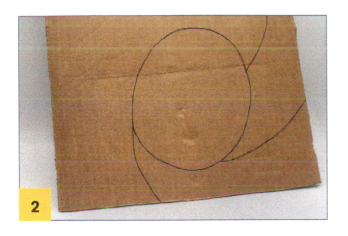

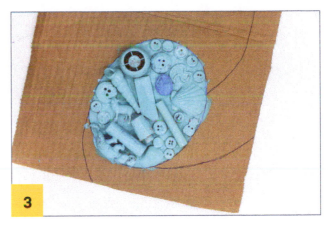

WHAT YOU DO:

1. Gather as many small objects as you can find and that your parents wouldn't mind you using for an art project. You can look outside for rocks and twigs, or even look around inside for some small toys or buttons. Anything goes for this project!

2. Draw a design onto the cardboard that you would like to create as a mosaic. This design can be a drawing of an object, or simply a pattern that you love.

3. Fill in your drawing by gluing the small found objects onto the design. Use either craft glue or hot glue (with the help of an adult) to secure each piece. Once you have one section filled in, paint the section using acrylic paint. Make sure you paint each piece, even down in the cracks, and let it dry.

4. Glue more found objects to fill in the next section and, once it's full, paint the section. Repeat this process for all other sections until your design is completely filled in.

5. Add a ribbon or pipe cleaner to the back of your piece with hot glue so that you can hang it on the wall.

Advanced Art

Create a mosaic frame for your mosaic. You can find old frames in thrift or junk stores, and you don't even need the glass. Collect additional found objects and glue them onto the frame. Paint the entire frame a color that you didn't use in your mosaic and insert your art.

Found Object-in-a-Box Assemblage

Messy Meter: ① ② ③ ④ ⑤

Assemblage sculptures are made by attaching found or made objects together to create something interesting. We'll be using some small found objects from your collection to design an assemblage to display.

by Matthew C.

WHAT YOU NEED:

* Five or six small boxes or lids, such as jewelry gift boxes
* Scrapbook paper
* Decoupage glue
* Sponge
* 11-by-14-inch piece of corrugated cardboard
* White paint or primer
* Paintbrushes
* Acrylic or tempera paint in colors of your choice
* Five or six small found objects from your collection
* Low-temp hot glue gun ⚠
* Hot glue sticks
* Ribbon or pipe cleaner

WHAT YOU DO:

1. Decorate each of your small boxes or lids using scrapbook paper. Tear small pieces of the papers you will use, then use a sponge to spread decoupage glue on the back of each piece before sticking them onto the inside of the box.

2. Paint both sides of your cardboard with white paint or primer to keep it from getting wavy. Let it dry, and then decorate one side with colorful paint, scrapbook paper, or both!

3. Glue each of your found objects into one of your boxes using hot glue (with an adult's help). You may choose to paint your objects before gluing them, but you don't have to if they already have interesting colors and patterns.

4. Place your boxes onto the cardboard background in the order that you would like them. Move them around until you think you have a great composition or arrangement. Ask an adult to glue your boxes onto the cardboard using hot glue.

5. Add a ribbon or pipe cleaner to the back of your cardboard with hot glue (with an adult's help), so that you can hang it on the wall.

Advanced Art

Add more details to your artwork by including a ribbon border, washi tape around your boxes, or creating a pattern with beads! Use craft glue to attach these items.

MORE FOUND OBJECT IDEAS

1. Make a silly character using found objects. Give it eyes, a funny nose, or maybe even arms and legs.

2. Make a mobile or hanging artwork out of found objects and string. Use a stick to tie everything onto.

3. Use an empty milk carton to create a miniature house, or a regular-size birdhouse! Cut out holes for windows and a door, then decorate the outside using scrapbook paper, paint, and other objects from your collection.

4. Use twigs you find outside to create letters by hot gluing them together. Wrap them with yarn or string after the glue dries to add color.

5. Use egg cartons to make a flower bouquet. Cut out each of the 12 sections, or cups, and turn them upside down. Cut petals along the edge using scissors. Paint each flower and add a stem using a stick or wire.

Chapter 6

Mixed Media

Mixed media art provides an awesome opportunity for artists of all skill levels to experiment and explore with lots of different materials. Painting, drawing, collage, paper cutting, and sculpture are just a few of the art techniques that you can use when creating a mixed media piece. There are no restrictions! Mixed media happens to be our favorite way to create art in our studio, because we love getting messy and going with the flow. Get your create space ready for some mess-making and bring your ideas to life.

> "Art is something that makes you breathe with a different kind of happiness."
>
> —Anni Albers

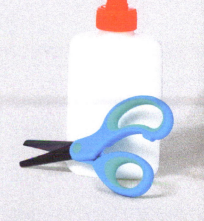

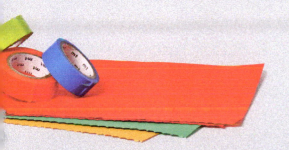

Mixed Media squares

Messy Meter: ① ② ③ ④ ⑤

You don't always have to have a plan when you start making a new piece of artwork. Sometimes you get inspired by the materials you're using to make something beautiful and interesting. That's exactly what this project is all about. There are no rules, except to be creative with the tools and colors you choose to work with.

by Maci C.

WHAT YOU NEED:

* Nine squares of 3-by-3-inch mixed media paper, any color
* 12-by-12-inch sheet of mixed media paper
* Scrapbook paper (or any decorative paper)
* Scissors
* Glue
* Washi tape
* Markers
* Pencil
* Eraser
* Glue stick

WHAT YOU DO:

1. Cut out small sections of scrapbook paper to glue to your squares. Choose patterns or pictures that you like. Your squares do not have to be all the same. In fact, it's better if they are different, yet still have some similar colors and elements mixed in. Don't worry if your papers are hanging off the edge of your squares; you can cut them off later.

2. Now add more to your squares by using washi tape. You could also draw right on top of your background, or you can draw on a white sheet of paper, cut it out, and glue it to a decorated square.

3. Once all of your squares are full, trim the edges, and arrange them on the 12-by-12-inch sheet of mixed media paper, three on each row. Pay attention to what colors you used in each square and spread them out, so your piece looks even and unified. Glue each square down to your background, making sure to leave space between each one.

Advanced Art

Use a marker or paint pen to create more designs on each of your squares. Using a little bit of one color (like white or gold) on each square will tie them all together.

Modern Self-Portrait

Messy Meter: ① ② ③ ④ ⑤

This project is all about you. First, you'll draw a picture of yourself without looking down at your paper. It's a technique called blind contour drawing. Then, you'll transform your self-portrait into a modern, mixed-media masterpiece.

Advanced Art

by Jade L.

WHAT YOU NEED:

* Mirror
* Mixed media or watercolor paper
* Pencil
* Black permanent marker
* Scrap cardboard
* Found objects (scrap paper, fabric, buttons, stickers, etc.)
* Craft glue

WHAT YOU DO:

1. Look at yourself in the mirror and decide which facial expression fits your personality best. Is it serious, silly, or a little of both?

2. Now create a few self-portraits through blind contour drawing. Start by placing the point of your pencil on your paper and choose which part of your face to start with. Draw slowly and "trace" your facial features in the mirror with your eyes as you go, being sure to look only

at what you are trying to draw and not at your paper. Don't forget smaller details, like your eyelashes, shirt collar, dimples in your cheeks, etc.

3. Choose one that you really like and outline it using a black permanent marker. Make sure you stay on the lines you created while drawing blind.

4. Cut out your self-portrait, but stay away from your lines so that you have an even border all the way around your drawing.

5. Now it's time for the background. Go on a scavenger hunt to find a variety of found objects in just one color to make it monochromatic. Glue the items you found onto a scrap piece of cardboard.

6. Attach your blind contour portrait to the background.

Advanced Art

Make a small stack of scrap squares of cardboard and glue them together. Glue the stack behind your self-portraits to make them pop and place them anywhere you would like on your background.

Cardboard Wall Art

Messy Meter: ① ② ③ ④ ⑤

We love creating artwork that has texture, especially when it's three-dimensional! In this project, we'll be layering pieces of corrugated cardboard (some with the top layer peeled away to reveal the texture underneath) to create an amazing textured wall hanging.

by Matthew C.

WHAT YOU NEED:

* Scrap pieces of corrugated cardboard
* Scissors
* Oil pastels or acrylic paint
* Paintbrushes
* Paint palette
* Cup of water
* Three 6-by-10-inch pieces of corrugated cardboard
* Low-temp hot glue gun ❗
* Hot glue sticks
* Hole punch
* String or yarn

WHAT YOU DO:

1. Cut the scrap cardboard pieces into interesting shapes. These shapes do not have to be perfect. Have some fun with it and cut out as many as you can.

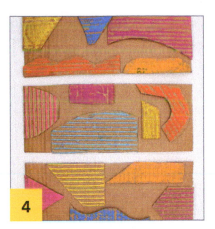

2. Peel off the top layer from some of the cutouts to reveal the bumpy texture underneath. This will give your piece a really interesting look with a lot of variety.

3. Using oil pastels or paint, add color to all of your cutouts and let them dry. You can use as many colors as you would like. We decided to stick with four colors: yellow, pink, orange, and blue.

4. Line up the three 6-by-10-inch pieces of cardboard vertically and lay the cutouts on top. Test out different combinations of shapes and colors. When you're happy with the placement, glue down your first layer of pieces to the three background pieces.

5. Create a second layer of cutouts on top of your first. Again, lay your pieces out before you start gluing to make sure you're happy.

6. Ask an adult to help you punch holes into each corner of the top two background pieces. Punch only the top two corners of the bottom background piece. Use yarn or string to tie each piece together, one on top of the other. Then tie a long strand at the top to hang it on the wall.

Advanced Art

Add a fourth layer to your wall hanging. Make four or five additional colored cutouts, or use leftovers from the main project, if you have any. Ask an adult to punch a hole at the top of each shape and then to punch a hole for every cutout along the bottom of the wall hanging. Tie a cutout to each hole along the bottom and enjoy your new fringe layer.

Mixed Media Photo Collage

Messy Meter: ② ③ ④

Sometimes artists get stuck and don't know what to draw or create. When that happens, it is important to know a few tricks to get your head back in the game. Creating a new drawing from an existing photo is a great way to get your brain moving and let your creativity flow.

WHAT YOU NEED:

* Magazines or photos
* Scissors
* 9-by-12-inch mixed media paper
* Glue stick
* Pencil
* Eraser
* Black permanent marker
* Colored pencils or markers

Advanced Art

Instead of using just one photo, try combining multiple photos of different objects, animals, or people in order to create something crazy and fun. A lion with a lady's head? A toaster with arms and legs? Why not! Feel free to add on to your creations as much as you want.

WHAT YOU DO:

1. Look through magazines or old photos (that you are allowed to cut) to find some interesting objects, animals, or faces.

2. Cut out as many as you would like and glue each one to a different sheet of mixed media paper. "Add on" to the cutouts by drawing additional things extending out from the photo. For example, if you found a face, you could add a funny body to it or a speech bubble. If you found an animal or creature, you could add more to its body or create a background.

3. Once your drawings are complete, outline them with a black permanent marker and then add color using colored pencils or markers for extra detail.

by Ozan H.

3-D Paper Scenes

Messy Meter: ① ② ③ ④ ⑤

Now that you've had some practice with two-dimensional and three-dimensional artwork, let's combine them. Here you will learn how to create a three-dimensional scene in a shadow box, using your own drawings on paper to make your ideas come to life.

by Matthew C.

WHAT YOU NEED:

* Four sheets of mixed media paper, small enough to fit inside a shoe box
* Pencil
* Eraser
* Markers or colored pencils
* Black permanent marker
* Scissors
* Craft glue
* Scrap cardboard pieces
* Acrylic or tempera paint
* Paintbrushes
* Shoe box

Advanced Art

Add one more layer of depth to your scene by painting the inside of the shoe box with a background scene *before* assembling your 3-D scene. This is an alternative to step 4.

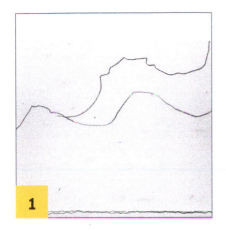

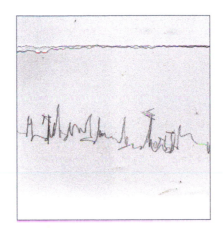

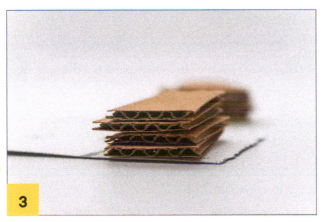

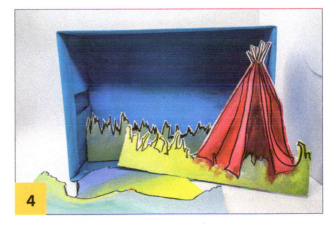

WHAT YOU DO:

1. Decide what kind of scene you want to create inside your box, and draw each item from your scene on a separate sheet of mixed media paper.

2. Use markers, colored pencils, or anything you want to add color to your drawings. Outline details with a black permanent marker so they are visible.

3. Cut out each piece. With craft glue, attach small pieces of cardboard stacked together onto the back of your drawings to help them stand up.

4. Paint the inside and the outside of your box using any colors you want to pair with your scene.

5. Once your box is dry, assemble your 3-D scene.

Stacked & Layered Foil Relief

Messy Meter: ① ② ③ ④ ⑤

Relief sculptures are a great way to bring dimension into your artwork. In this project, you will be mixing your painting skills with a low-relief sculpture to create a beautiful, shiny piece of artwork for your wall.

by Maci C.

WHAT YOU NEED:

* Masking tape
* 5-by-5-inch piece of corrugated cardboard
* 12-by-12-inch or larger mixed media paper
* Pencil
* Eraser
* Acrylic or tempera paint
* Paintbrushes
* Cup of water
* Paint palette
* Black permanent marker
* Craft glue
* Yarn
* Scissors
* Aluminum foil
* Spray adhesive (optional)
* Colored markers

1

3

4

WHAT YOU DO:

1. Cut a piece of masking tape and double it over to create a sticky roll. Stick it to the back of your cardboard to temporarily attach it to the mixed media paper. With your two pieces attached, draw your picture, design, or pattern with a pencil, being sure to overlap it onto your cardboard piece.

2. Carefully lift the cardboard from the mixed media paper. Paint the design with acrylic or tempera paint. Once it's dry, outline your design with black permanent marker.

3. On the cardboard piece, "trace" over each pencil line with craft glue, and then add yarn right on top of the glue lines.

4. Cut a piece of aluminum foil, slightly larger than your cardboard, and smooth it onto the surface. You will notice the lines of yarn creating bumps under the foil. Be careful not to scratch the foil as you rub. (Optional: Cover your cardboard with spray adhesive before adding foil.) Use markers to color your shiny relief.

5. Use craft glue to attach the relief to your painted background.

Advanced Art

Attach a piece of paper that is bigger than 12-by-12-inches, to the back of your artwork to add an extra layer. Use a different medium to fill in your pattern.

2-D Paper Puppets

Messy Meter: ① ② ③ ④ ⑤

Have you ever wished that your artwork could move? Well, with the right mix of materials, it can do just that. Let's create a "character" that can move around its environment, even in a two-dimensional form.

by Matthew C.

WHAT YOU NEED:

* 11-by-14-inch sheet of mixed media paper
* Pencil
* Eraser
* Colored pencils or markers
* 5-by-7-inch sheet of mixed media paper
* Black permanent marker
* Scissors
* Craft knife ❗
* Craft stick or small dowel rod
* Glue stick

WHAT YOU DO:

1. Think about what you would like to make move and its environment. It can be anything. We chose a pencil and a sharpener. On the larger sheet of paper, draw the background, or environment, for your "character." Add color.

2. Draw the character or object on the smaller sheet of paper. Outline the drawing with a black permanent marker to help it stand out, then use pencils or markers to fill the rest in with color.

3. Cut out your character and glue a craft stick to the back of it.

4. Look at your background and decide where you would like your character to be. It will be able to move up and down and side to side, so make sure you choose a spot where your character will have plenty of room. Ask an adult to help you cut a slit in your paper with the craft knife exactly where you'd like your character to pop into the environment.

5. Slide your character through the slit, and move it around by holding the stick from behind your paper!

Advanced Art

Complete the back of your character so you can twirl it around in its environment.

Create Your Own Sketchbook

Messy Meter: ① ② ③ ④ ⑤

Instead of making all your artwork on separate pieces of paper, making art in a sketchbook that you can carry with you is a totally different experience. You may think about how the artwork you create inside your sketchbook relates to each other or works together, and you may even be inspired to draw while you're on the go!

by Maci C.

WHAT YOU NEED:

* Six or more 12-by-18-inch sheets of mixed media or drawing paper
* Hole punch
* Cereal box
* Scissors
* Yarn or string
* Markers
* Pens
* Washi tape
* Found objects

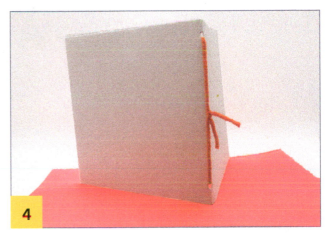

WHAT YOU DO:

1. Fold all of your 12-by-18-inch papers in half on the long side to make multiple 9-by-12-inch book pages.

2. Place three folded pieces together and, using a hole punch, punch two half-circle holes right on the fold. Do the same for the rest of your folded pieces, making sure to do it in the same place on each one. Stack all of your papers together, lining up the holes you punch on the folds.

3. Add a sturdy cover to your sketchbook using a recycled cereal box. Have an adult cut the box open and trim it to 12.5-by-18.5-inches. Fold it in half and punch holes that align with the ones on the paper.

4. Use yarn or string to tie all of your pieces together. Lace it through the top hole, and then back out of the bottom hole. Tie a sturdy knot or bow on the outside of your book.

5. Decorate your cover with color, washi tape, and leftover scrapbook paper to create a collage. Glue found objects from your collection to make it even more special.

Advanced Art

Add an inner pocket to your sketchbook. Ask an adult to cut out a 6-by-9-inch rectangle from the remainder of the cereal box. Use a stapler to attach it to the inner front cover and use the pocket to store loose papers.

MORE MIXED MEDIA IDEAS

1. Make a large aluminum foil relief.

2. Carry your sketchbook with you and challenge yourself to make five drawings or sketches in one day.

3. Create a miniature 3-D paper scene using a matchbox.

4. Create an animal that has moving parts. Draw and cut out each part of the animal and then attach its legs, arms, head, and tail with small brads so you can move each piece.

5. Use tissue paper and decoupage glue to create a collage. If you do it on glass or another clear surface, it will look like stained glass.

GLOSSARY

Additive sculpture: a sculptural technique where you combine materials

Blind contour drawing: creating an image without looking at your paper

Collaboration: working together with other people

Complementary: colors that are opposites on the color wheel

Composition: an arrangement of the visual elements in a work of art

Contour line drawing: creating an image of something by only drawing its outline

Cubism: a style of art where painters used simple geometric shapes to paint their subject

Decoupage: using glue to paste items, such as paper, onto a surface

Depth: how close or far things appear in a piece of artwork

Dimension: the measurable size of something

Focal point: the part of your artwork that stands out the most

Geometric shapes: objects that have uniform measurements and don't often appear in nature

Hatched lines: closely-spaced parallel lines

Highlights: a spot in a painting or a drawing that looks bright

Horizontal: going from left to right, or sideways

Illustration: art that tells a story

Loom: the base from which you create a weaving

Monochromatic: something that is all one color

Monoprint: a way to create a one-of-a-kind image by transferring color to a surface

Mosaics: a style of art where small pieces of colored glass are combined to form an image

Negative space: the space around an object, or the background of an artwork

Oil pastels: coloring sticks made from oil, wax, and other ingredients

Organic shapes: shapes that can be found in nature and that are smooth and flowing, not geometric

Overlap: the placement of objects so that one covers another and creates the illusion of depth

Painterly: the look of visible brushstrokes in an art piece

Panel painting: art created on multiple pieces of wood and then connected or displayed together to tell a story

Papier-mâché: a mixture used as a paste to create a hard layer on a sculpture

Pointillism: drawing or painting using only dots

Primer: a preparatory coat on a surface

Printmaking: creating an image by applying ink to one surface and then transferring that ink onto another surface

Relief: a sculpture technique where three-dimensional elements are raised above a flat background

Scale: the size of an object when compared to other objects

Shades: a mixture of a color with black to increase darkness

Stencil: a surface (such as paper or cardboard) with shapes cut out of the center used to print or trace those shapes onto another surface

Still life: a collection of objects that has been set up so that you can draw or paint their image

Subtractive sculpture: a sculptural technique where you take away pieces of your material instead of adding to it

Symmetrical: a perfect balance, or when two halves match perfectly

Texture: how something feels, or how it looks like it feels (for example, bumpy, sharp, wavy, smooth, etc.)

Three-dimensional: having volume

Tints: a mixture of a color with white to decrease darkness

Two-dimensional: flat, or without volume

Variety: adding interest to a work of art by placing different elements next to each other

Vertical: going up and down

Warp: the part of a weaving that goes from top to bottom

Weaving: a way to create fabric by connecting yarn or string

Weft: the part of a weaving that goes from side to side

RESOURCES

PLACES TO BUY SUPPLIES

Walmart

Hobby Lobby

Michaels

JOANN Fabrics

ARTISTS TO CHECK OUT

Alexander Calder
an American sculptor best known for innovative mobiles

Marcel Duchamp
a French-American painter and sculptor well-known for found objects

Albrecht Dürer
a German painter and printmaker well-known for engravings, a style of printmaking

Jasper Johns
an American painter, sculptor, and printmaker well-known for hatched lines

Hannah Höch
a German artist best known for photomontage and collage

Paul Klee
a Swiss artist best known for painting, drawing, watercolor, and printmaking

Michelangelo
an Italian Renaissance painter, sculptor, and architect well-known for subtractive sculptures

Pablo Picasso
a Spanish painter, sculptor, and printmaker well-known for Cubism

Rembrandt
a Dutch painter and printmaker who produced etchings, a form of printmaking

Georges Seurat
a French post-Impressionist painter best known for developing the technique of pointillism

Vincent Van Gogh
a Dutch post-Impressionist painter well-known for still life, landscapes, and self-portraits

Andy Warhol
an American printmaker and painter, well-known for silkscreens, a type of printmaking

INDEX

ABOUT THE AUTHORS

Daniel and Korri Freeman are working artists and art teachers in Russellville, Arkansas. They own and run a business out of their cozy downtown studio and art gallery. Daniel creates artwork and has regular art shows in the gallery, while Korri teaches art classes, hosts children's art events, and runs summer camps. You can always find them with their daughter, Finnli, at the KaleidoKids Art Studio creating, making, and having fun! To find out more about their work visit kaleidokidsart.com or follow them on Facebook and Instagram: @kaleidokidsart.

CPSIA information can be obtained
at www.ICGtesting.com
Printed in the USA
BVHW052201231119
564441BV00007B/57